MON CAHIER D'ÉCRITURE

J'APPRENDS À LIRE ET À ÉCRIRE MONTESSORI

My Sight Word List

French - Serbian

a	in	said
and	is	see
away	it	the
big	jump	three
blue	little	to
can	look	two
come	make	up
down	me	we
find	my	where
for	not	yellow
funny	one	you
go	day	
help	play	
here	red	
I	run	

Name: ____________________ Date: ____________________

Today is: Monday | Tuesday | Wednesday | Thursday | Friday

Direction: Trace and read the sentences.

amusement	pistolet	courir	soleil
	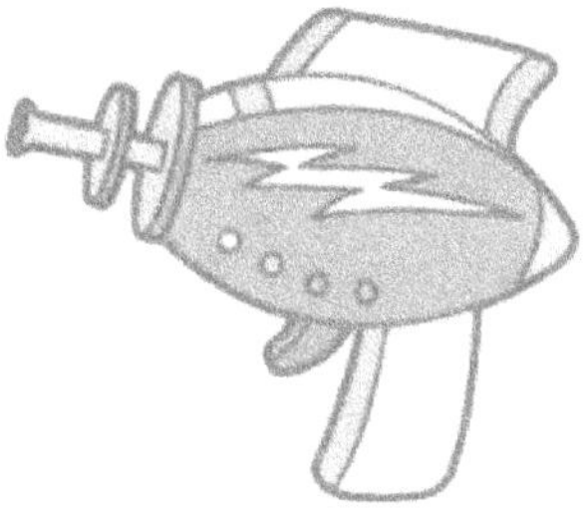		
забавно	пиштољ	трцати	сунце

They are having fun.

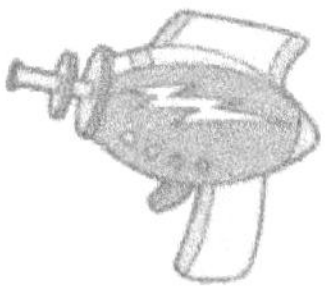

He has a gun.

The bear is running.

The sun is smiling.

Draw a Picture

I Can...

- [ ] use a Capital Letter
  The cat is big.
- [ ] use spaces
- [ ] sound out words
  d-o-g = dog
- [ ] use a Period .
- [ ] Draw a picture

He is having fun, running under the sun with his new toy gun.

amusement	pistolet	courir	soleil
забавно	пиштољ	трцати	сунце

Name: _________________ Date: _________

Today is:

| Monday | Tuesday | Wednesday |
| Thursday | Friday |

Direction: Trace and read the sentences.

sac	chiffon	étiquette	remuer
кеса	крпе	таг	махање

He has many bags.

I see a rag.

I see a tag.

Its tail is wagging.

Draw a Picture

I Can...

use a Capital Letter
The cat is big.

use spaces

sound out words
d-o-g = dog

use a Period .

Draw a
picture

The bag on the rag has a blue tag which made the dog's tail wag.

sac	chiffon	étiquette	remuer
кеса	крпе	таг	махање

Name: _______________ Date: _______________

Today is: | Monday | | Tuesday | | Wednesday |
| Thursday | | Friday |

Direction: Trace and read the sentences.

| canettes | homme | la poêle | van |
| конзерва | човек | пан | комби |

I see a can of soda.

The man is happy.

The pan is dirty.

I see a big van.

The man who was driving a van ran over a can and a pan.

Name: _________________________ Date: _______________

Today is: | Monday | Tuesday | Wednesday |
| Thursday | Friday |

Direction: Trace and read the sentences.

| couper | intestin | cabane | écrou |
| исећи | црева | колиба | орах |

He cut his nails.

He has a gut.

This is a small hut.

It is holding a nut.

Name

Draw a Picture

I Can...

- [ ] use a Capital Letter
  <u>T</u>he cat is big.

- [ ] use spaces

- [ ] sound out words
  d-o-g = dog

- [ ] use a Period .

- [ ] Draw a picture

A boy swallowed a nut and it got stuck in his belly. He had to get his gut cut open in the hut.

couper	intestin	cabane	écrou
исећи	црева	колиба	орах

Name: ____________________ Date: ____________________

Today is: Monday | Tuesday | Wednesday | Thursday | Friday

Direction: Trace and read the sentences.

graisse	chat	chapeau	tapis

дебео	мачка	шешир	мат

I see a fat dog.

This is my little cat.

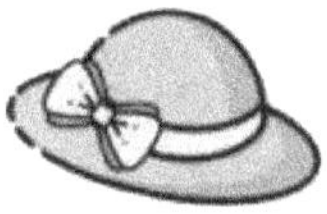

I like this hat.

I see a big mat.

Draw a Picture

I Can...

- [ ] use a Capital Letter
  The cat is big.

- [ ] use spaces

- [ ] sound out words
  d-o-g = dog

- [ ] use a Period .

- [ ] Draw a picture

The fat cat laid on the mat that was a hat pattern.

graisse	chat	chapeau	tapis
дебео	мачка	шешир	мат

Name: _______________________ Date: _______________

Today is: | Monday | Tuesday | Wednesday |
| Thursday | Friday |

Direction: Trace and read the sentences.

taxi	laboratoire	languette	crabe
такси	лабораторија	картицу	краба

The cab is fast.

The lab is exciting.

The tab is long.

We found a crab.

Draw a Picture

I Can...

- [ ] use a Capital Letter
  The cat is big.
- [ ] use spaces
- [ ] sound out words
  d-o-g = dog
- [ ] use a Period .
- [ ] Draw a picture

The crab called a cab to drive him to the lab and when he got off he paid his tab.

taxi	laboratoire	languette	crabe
такси	лабораторија	картицу	краба

Name: ____________________ Date: ____________________

Today is: Monday | Tuesday | Wednesday | Thursday | Friday

Direction: Trace and read the sentences.

jambon	confiture	mouton	palourde
		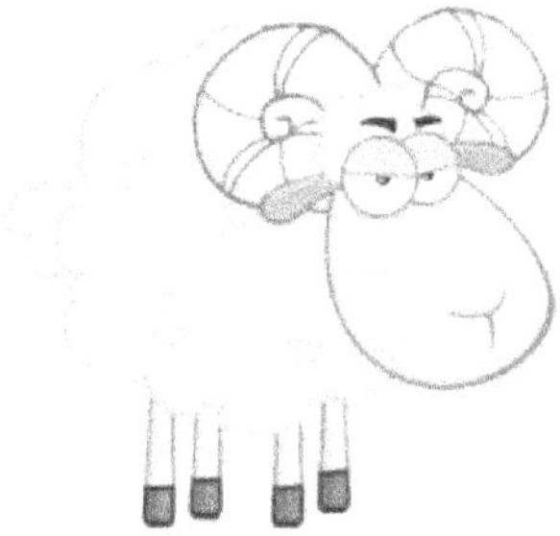	
шунка	џем	овце	шкољка

I like to eat ham.

We like to eat jam.

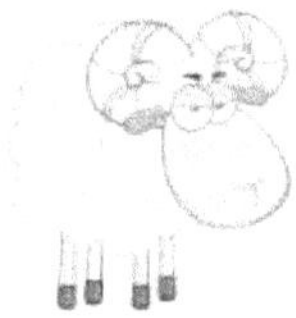
The ram is big.

The clam is pretty.

The clam gave the ram ham. Then the ram gave the clam jam.

jambon	confiture	mouton	palourde
шунка	џем	овце	шкољка

Name: ______________________ Date: ______________________

Today is: Monday Tuesday Wednesday Thursday Friday

Direction: Trace and read the sentences.

lit	de premier plan	rouge	mariage
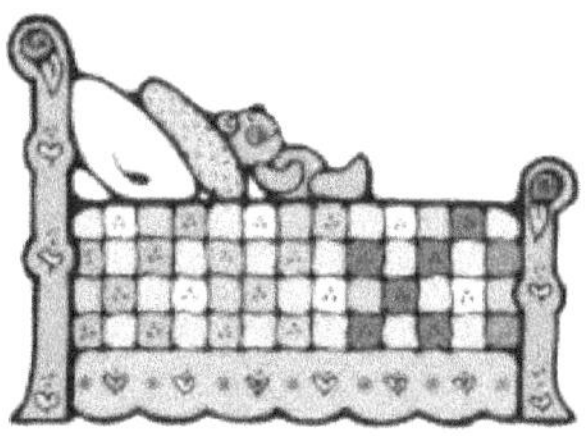			
кревет	водећи	црвено	венчање

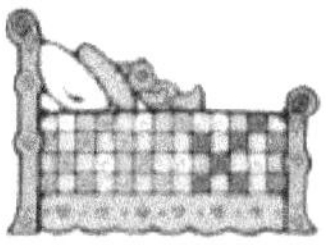 This is my little bed.

 He led us to safety.

 The apple is red.

 He asks her to wed.

Name

Draw a Picture

I Can...

- [ ] use a Capital Letter
  The cat is big.

- [ ] use spaces

- [ ] sound out words
  d-o-g = dog

- [ ] use a Period .

- [ ] Draw a picture

When the prince got out of bed, he was led on a red carpet to be wed with the princess.

lit	de premier plan	rouge	mariage
кревет	водећи	црвено	венчање

Name: ______________________ Date: ______________________

Today is: Monday | Tuesday | Wednesday | Thursday | Friday

Direction: Trace and read the sentences.

mauvais	papa	furieux	triste
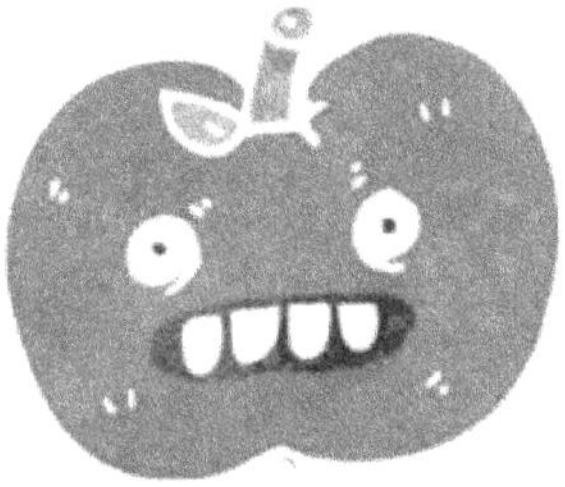	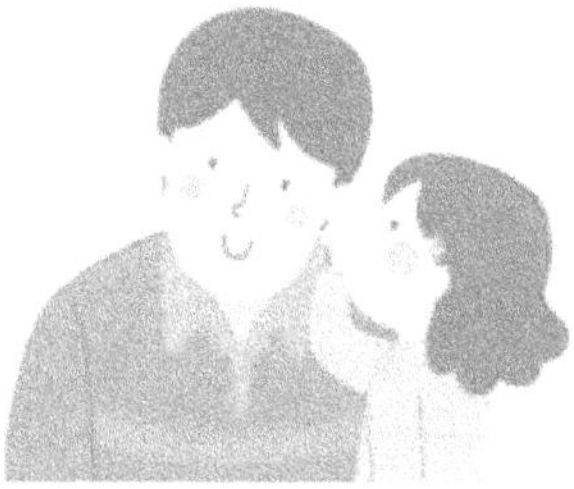	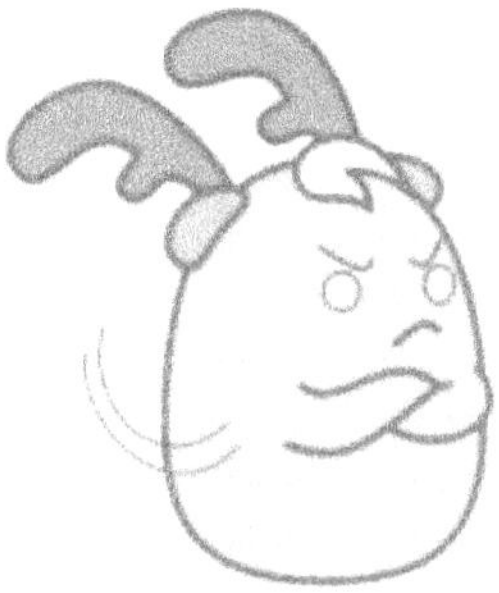	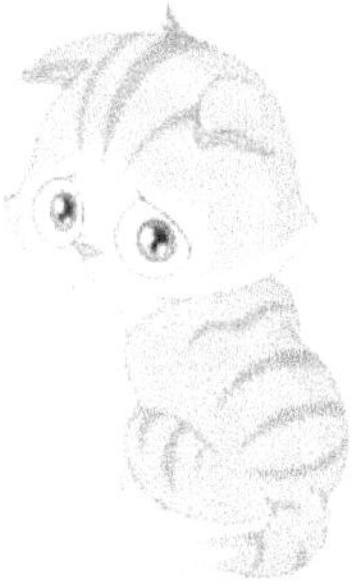
лоше	тата	луд	тузно

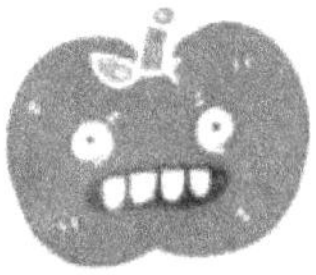

This apple is bad.

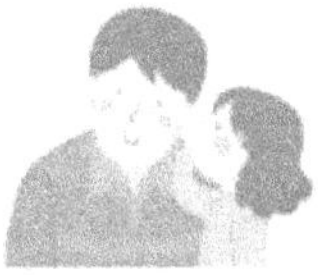

My dad is very kind.

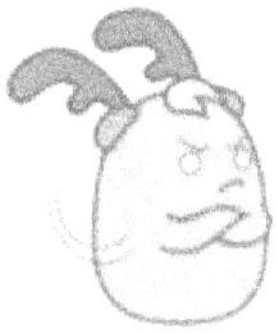

The reindeer is mad.

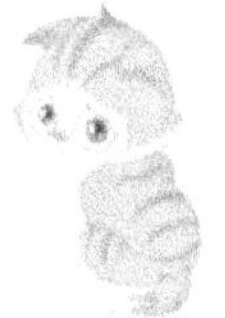

The little cat is sad.

Draw a Picture

I Can...

- [ ] use a Capital Letter
  <u>T</u>he cat is big.
- [ ] use spaces
- [ ] sound out words
  d-o-g = dog
- [ ] use a Period .
- [ ] Draw a picture

I was bad so my dad got mad and now I am so sad.

mauvais	papa	furieux	triste
лоше	тата	луд	тузно

Name: _________________________ Date: _______________

Today is: [Monday] [Tuesday] [Wednesday]
          [Thursday] [Friday]

Direction: Trace and read the sentences.

animal den	poule	écuries	dix
ден	кокошка	стаје	десет

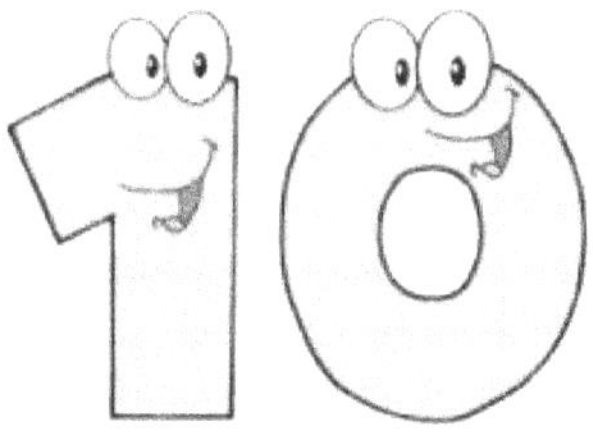

It is a den.

The hens lay eggs.

She has a good pen.

The ten is smiling.

Draw a Picture

I Can...

- [ ] use a Capital Letter
  The cat is big.
- [ ] use spaces
- [ ] sound out words
  d-o-g = dog
- [ ] use a Period .
- [ ] Draw a picture

The hen that lived in the pen laid ten eggs in her den.

animal den	poule	écuries	dix
ден	кокошка	стаје	десет

Name: ____________________ Date: ____________________

Today is: Monday | Tuesday | Wednesday | Thursday | Friday

Direction: Trace and read the sentences.

gommeux	maman	somme	tambour

гуми	мама	сума	бубањ

 I like to chew gum.

 My mum is kind!

 I can do a sum!

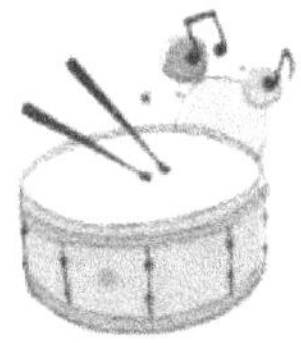 The drum is big.

Draw a Picture

I Can...

- [ ] use a Capital Letter
  The cat is big.

- [ ] use spaces

- [ ] sound out words
  d-o-g = dog

- [ ] use a Period .

- [ ] Draw a picture

Mum was chewing gum while figuring out the sum of the drum's price.

gommeux	maman	somme	tambour
гуми	мама	сума	бубањ

Name: ______________________ Date: ______________________

Today is: Monday | Tuesday | Wednesday | Thursday | Friday

Direction: Trace and read the sentences.

offre	cacher	enfant	couvercle
			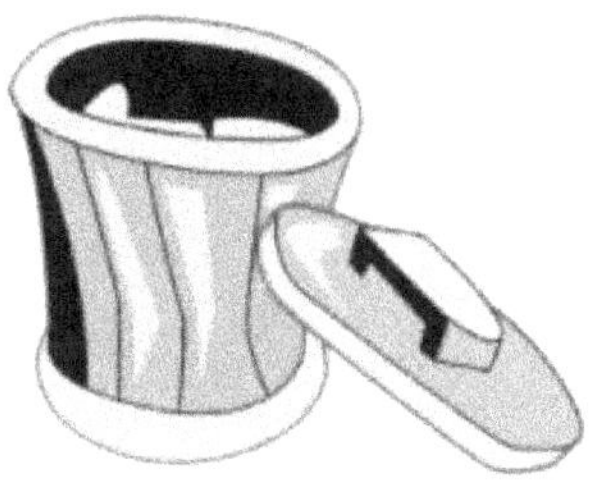
понуда	сакрити	дете	поклопац

 He likes to bid.

 He is hiding.

 The kid like to play.

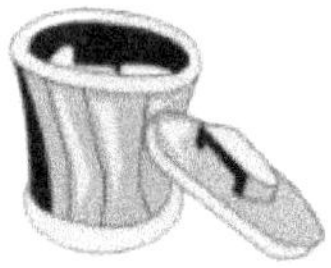 I see a lid.

Name

Draw a Picture

I Can...

- [ ] use a Capital Letter
  The cat is big.

- [ ] use spaces

- [ ] sound out words
  d-o-g = dog

- [ ] use a Period .

- [ ] Draw a picture

The kid bid a lid for one hundred dollars then hid from his mad parents.

offre	cacher	enfant	couvercle
понуда	сакрити	дете	поклопац

Name: ______________________ Date: ______________________

Today is: Monday | Tuesday | Wednesday | Thursday | Friday

Direction: Trace and read the sentences.

gros	creuser	porc	perruque
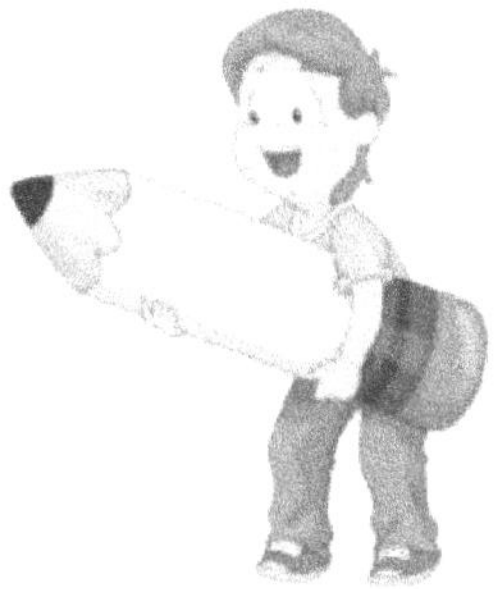	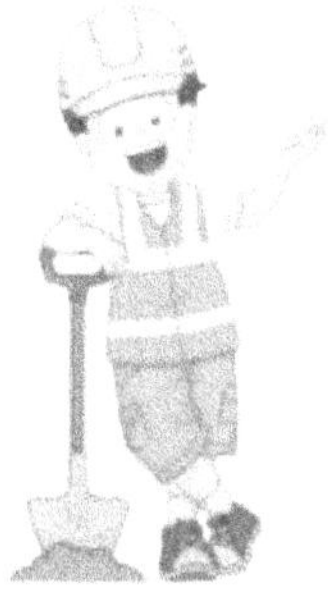	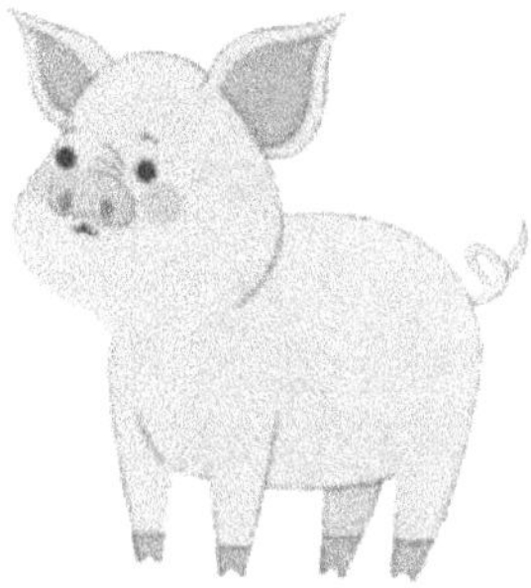	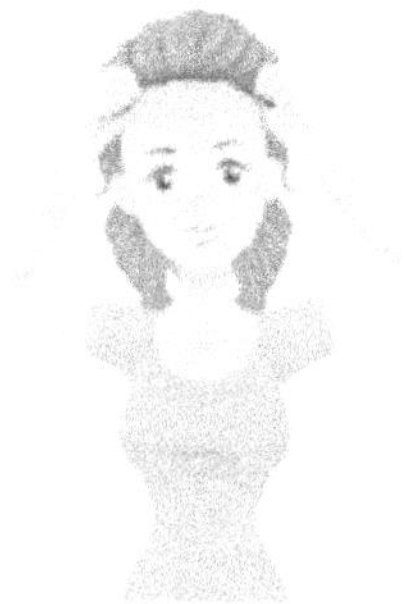
велика	копати	свиња	перика

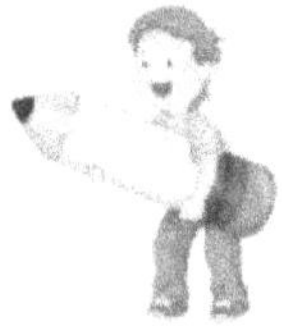

That is a big pencil.

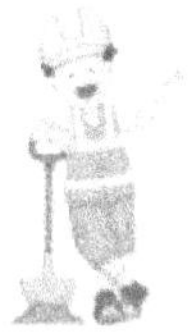

He will dig up a hole.

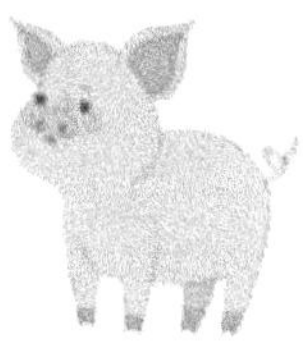

The pig is fat.

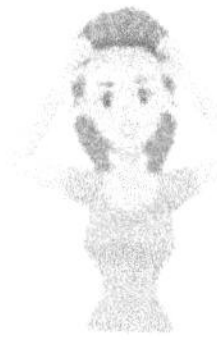

She puts on a wig.

Draw a Picture

I Can...

use a Capital Letter
The cat is big.

use spaces

sound out words
d-o-g = dog

use a Period .

Draw a
picture

The big pig went to dig
in the mud for his wig.

gros	creuser	porc	perruque
велика	копати	свиња	перика

Name: ____________________ Date: ____________________

Today is: Monday | Tuesday | Wednesday | Thursday | Friday

Direction: Trace and read the sentences.

poubelle	ailette	épingle	gagner
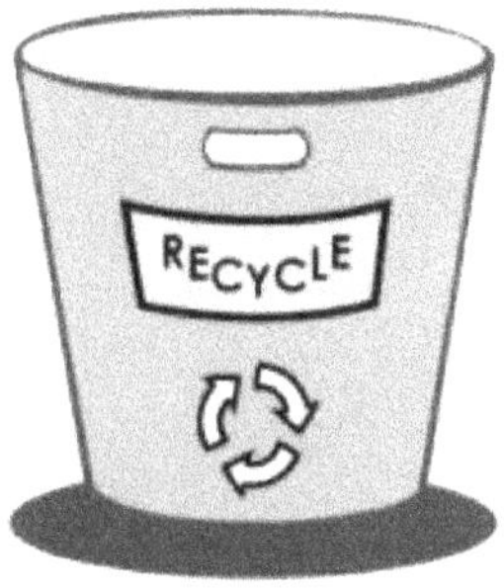	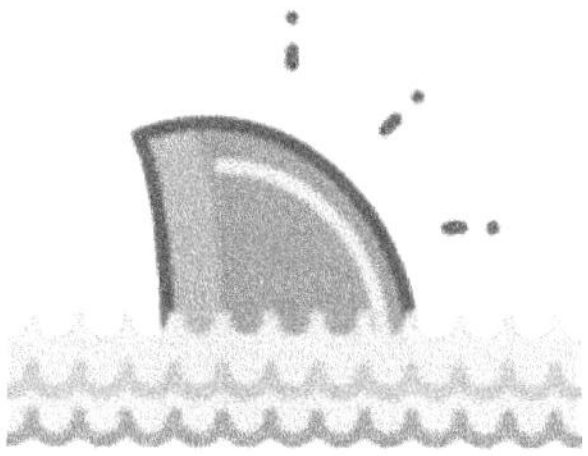	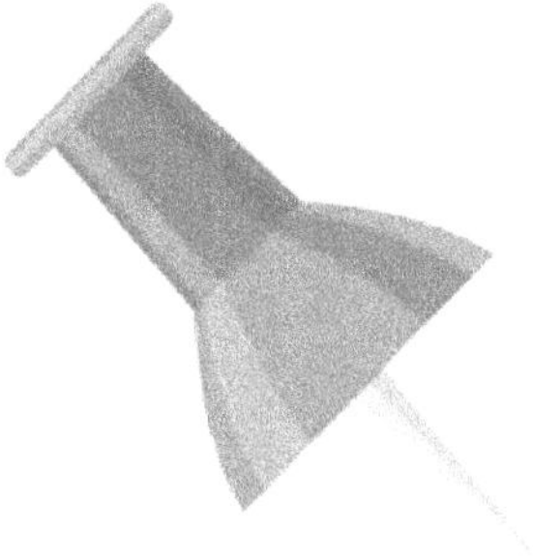	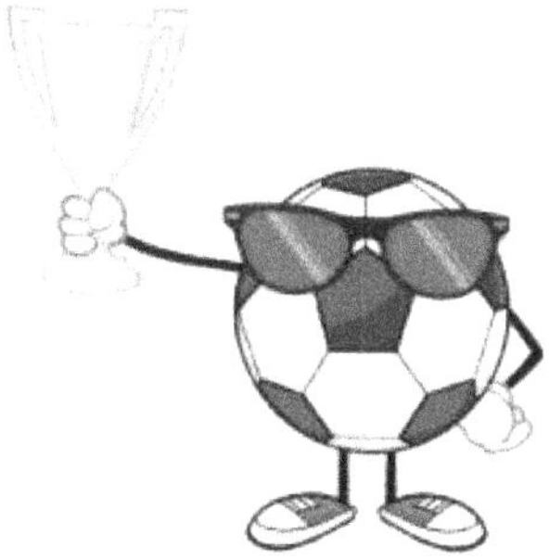
канта	перајa	пин	победити

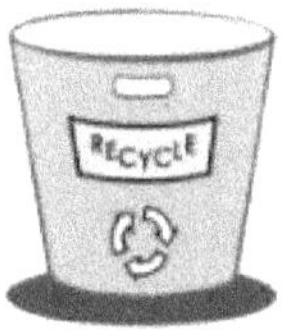
It is a recycle bin.

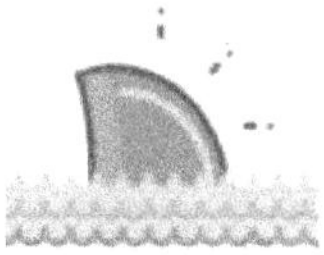
The shark has a fin.

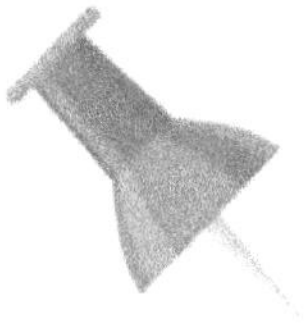
The pin is pointy.

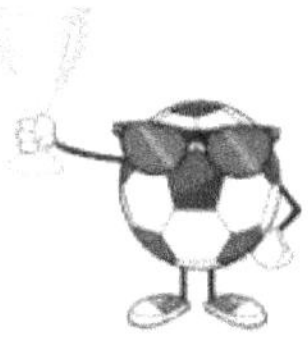
He won the match.

Draw a Picture

I Can...

- [ ] use a Capital Letter
  The cat is big.
- [ ] use spaces
- [ ] sound out words
  d-o-g = dog
- [ ] use a Period .
- [ ] Draw a picture

The dangerous fin of the fish was pinned to the bin. Then the sailors had a contest on who will win by touching the fin the longest.

poubelle	ailette	épingle	gagner
канта	пераја	пин	победити

Name: ____________________ Date: ____________________

Today is: Monday | Tuesday | Wednesday | Thursday | Friday

Direction: Trace and read the sentences.

hanche	lèvres	pincer	boisson

кука	усне	нип	пиће

This is my hip.

Her lips are red.

It is nipping its toy.

She is sipping.

Name

Draw a Picture

I Can...

- [ ] use a Capital Letter
  The cat is big.

- [ ] use spaces

- [ ] sound out words
  d-o-g = dog

- [ ] use a Period .

- [ ] Draw a picture

The dog nipped someone who was sipping water with his lip.

hanche	lèvres	pincer	boisson
кука	усне	нип	пиђе

Name: ______________________ Date: ______________________

Today is: Monday Tuesday Wednesday Thursday Friday

Direction: Trace and read the sentences.

en forme	frappé	trousse	asseoir
		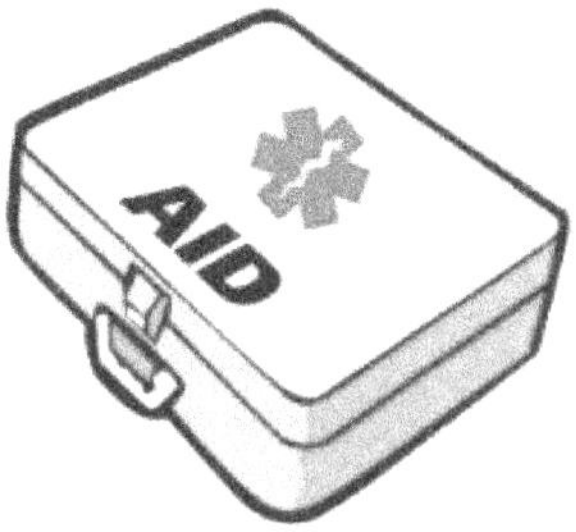	
стане	хит	кит	седи

It is perfectly fit.

They hit each other.

That is a safety kit.

He is sitting.

Name ______________________

Draw a Picture

I Can...

- [ ] use a Capital Letter
  The cat is big.
- [ ] use spaces
- [ ] sound out words
  d-o-g = dog
- [ ] use a Period .
- [ ] Draw a picture

The fit doctor sat then was hit by a kit.

en forme	frappé	trousse	asseoir
		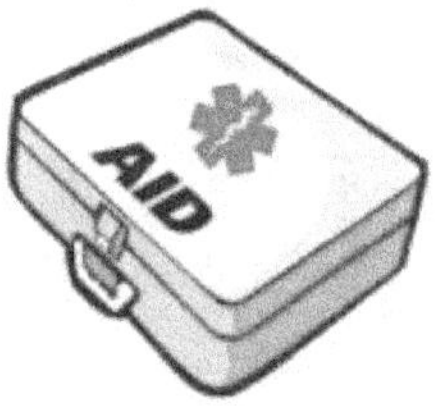	
стане	хит	кит	седи

Name: ____________________ Date: ____________________

Today is: Monday | Tuesday | Wednesday | Thursday | Friday

Direction: Trace and read the sentences.

blé	emploi	rob	pleurer

кукуруз	посао	опљачкати	плакати

 I ate corn on the cob.

 This is my job.

 He is robbing.

 The girl is sobbing.

Draw a Picture

I Can...

- ☐ use a Capital Letter
  <u>T</u>he cat is big.
- ☐ use spaces
- ☐ sound out words
  d-o-g = dog
- ☐ use a Period .
- ☐ Draw a picture

The chef robbed a corn cob and then was sobbing because he had lost his job.

blé	emploi	rob	pleurer
кукуруз	посао	опљачкати	плакати

Name: ______________________ Date: ______________________

Today is: Monday | Tuesday | Wednesday | Thursday | Friday

Direction: Trace and read the sentences.

chien	porc	le jogging	bois
			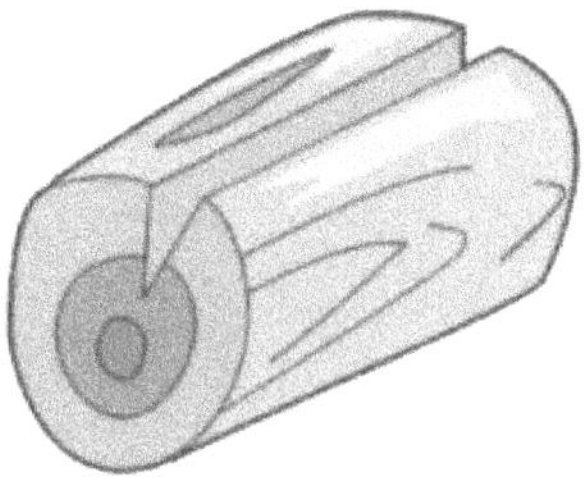
пас	свиња	јоггинг	дрво

The dog is thrilled.

The hog is big.

She is jogging.

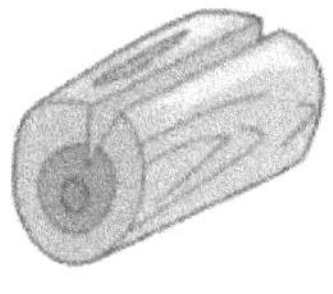

The log is small.

Name

Draw a Picture

I Can...

☐ use a Capital Letter
<u>T</u>he cat is big.

☐ use spaces

☐ sound out words
d-o-g = dog

☐ use a Period .

☐ Draw a
picture

The dog and the hog
went for a jog but then
tripped on a log.

chien	porc	le jogging	bois
пас	свиња	јоггинг	дрво

Name: _______________________ Date: _______________________

Today is: Monday   Tuesday   Wednesday
           Thursday   Friday

Direction: Trace and read the sentences.

punaise	étreinte	cruche	agresser
буг	загрлити	врч	шоља

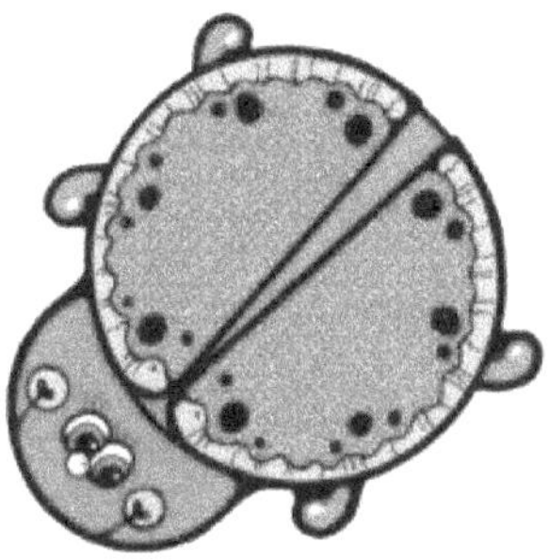

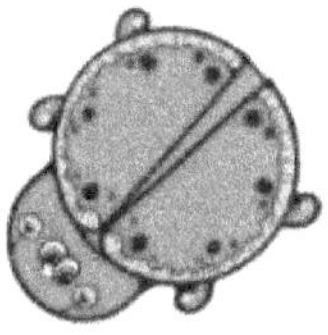

The bug is colorful.

She is hugging.

The jug has milk in it.

He has a mug.

Draw a Picture

I Can...

- [ ] use a Capital Letter
  The cat is big.
- [ ] use spaces
- [ ] sound out words
  d-o-g = dog
- [ ] use a Period .
- [ ] Draw a picture

The bug hugged the jug and the mug which was full of jam.

punaise	étreinte	cruche	agresser
буг	загрлити	врч	шоља

Name: _________________________ Date: _______________

Today is: [Monday] [Tuesday] [Wednesday]
[Thursday] [Friday]

Direction: Trace and read the sentences.

lit	point	chaud	pot
кревет	тачка	вруће	лонац

This is my cot.

There are many dots.

It is very hot.

He has a plant pot.

Name

Draw a Picture

I Can...

☐ use a Capital Letter
<u>T</u>he cat is big.

☐ use spaces

☐ sound out words
d-o-g = dog

☐ use a Period .

☐ Draw a picture

The baby climbed out of the cot with the dot pattern and ate the hot pot.

lit	point	chaud	pot
кревет	тачка	вруће	лонац

Direction: Read the words and make a sentence.

amusement	pistolet	courir	soleil
забавно	пиштољ	трцати	сунце

Name

Draw a Picture

I Can...

☐ use a Capital Letter
The cat is big.

☐ use spaces

☐ sound out words
d-o-g = dog

☐ use a Period .

☐ Draw a picture

Name: ___________________ Date: ___________________

Today is:

| Monday | Tuesday | Wednesday |

| Thursday | Friday |

Name: _________________________ Date: _________________________

Today is: Monday Tuesday Wednesday

Thursday Friday

Direction: Read the words and make a sentence.

sac	chiffon	étiquette	remuer
кеса	крпе	таг	махање

Name _______________________

Draw a Picture

I Can...

- [ ] use a Capital Letter
  The cat is big.

- [ ] use spaces

- [ ] sound out words
  d-o-g = dog

- [ ] use a Period .

- [ ] Draw a picture

Name: _______________________ Date: _______________

Today is: [Monday] [Tuesday] [Wednesday]
          [Thursday] [Friday]

Name: _______________________ Date: _______________

Today is: | Monday | Tuesday | Wednesday |
| Thursday | Friday |

Direction: Read the words and make a sentence.

| canettes | homme | la poêle | van |
| конзерва | човек | пан | комби |

Name

Draw a Picture

I Can...

☐ use a Capital Letter
The cat is big.

☐ use spaces

☐ sound out words
d-o-g = dog

☐ use a Period .

☐ Draw a
picture

Name:

Date:

Today is: Monday Tuesday Wednesday Thursday Friday

Name: ____________________ Date: ____________________

Today is: Monday Tuesday Wednesday Thursday Friday

Direction: Read the words and make a sentence.

couper	**intestin**	**cabane**	**écrou**

исећи	црева	колиба	орах

Name ____________________________

<table>
<tr><td>

Draw a Picture

</td><td>

I Can...

☐ use a Capital Letter
The cat is big.

☐ use spaces

☐ sound out words
d-o-g = dog

☐ use a Period .

☐ Draw a picture

</td></tr>
</table>

Name:
Date:
Today is:
Monday
Tuesday
Wednesday
Thursday
Friday

Name: _________________________ Date: _______________

Today is: [Monday] [Tuesday] [Wednesday]
           [Thursday] [Friday]

Direction: Read the words and make a sentence.

graisse	chat	chapeau	tapis
дебео	мачка	шешир	мат

Name

Draw a Picture

I Can...

- [ ] use a Capital Letter
  The cat is big.

- [ ] use spaces

- [ ] sound out words
  d-o-g = dog

- [ ] use a Period .

- [ ] Draw a picture

Name: _______________________ Date: _______________________

Today is: | Monday | Tuesday | Wednesday |

| Thursday | Friday |

Name: _________________________ Date: _______________

Today is: Monday   Tuesday   Wednesday

Thursday   Friday

Direction: Read the words and make a sentence.

taxi	laboratoire	languette	crabe
такси	лабораторија	картицу	краба

Draw a Picture

I Can...

- ☐ use a Capital Letter
  The cat is big.
- ☐ use spaces
- ☐ sound out words
  d-o-g = dog
- ☐ use a Period .
- ☐ Draw a picture

Name: _________________________ Date: _______________

Today is: Monday Tuesday Wednesday Thursday Friday

Name: _______________________ Date: _______________

Today is: [Monday] [Tuesday] [Wednesday]
[Thursday] [Friday]

Direction: Read the words and make a sentence.

jambon	confiture	mouton	palourde
шунка	џем	овце	шкољка

Name _______________________

Draw a Picture

I Can...

- ☐ use a Capital Letter
  The cat is big.

- ☐ use spaces

- ☐ sound out words
  d-o-g = dog

- ☐ use a Period .

- ☐ Draw a picture

Name: _______________   Date: _______________

Today is: [Monday] [Tuesday] [Wednesday]
           [Thursday] [Friday]

Name: ___________________ Date: ___________

Today is: | Monday | Tuesday | Wednesday |
| Thursday | Friday |

Direction: Read the words and make a sentence.

lit	**de premier plan**	**rouge**	**mariage**
кревет	водећи	црвено	венчање

____

____

____

____

Draw a Picture

I Can...

use a Capital Letter
The cat is big.

use spaces

sound out words
d-o-g = dog

use a Period .

Draw a
picture

Name: ___________________ Date: ___________________

Today is: Monday Tuesday Wednesday Thursday Friday

Name: ___________________ Date: _______________

Today is: Monday Tuesday Wednesday

Thursday Friday

Direction: Read the words and make a sentence.

mauvais	papa	furieux	triste
лоше	тата	луд	тузно

Name

Draw a Picture

I Can...

- [ ] use a Capital Letter
  The cat is big.

- [ ] use spaces

- [ ] sound out words
  d-o-g = dog

- [ ] use a Period .

- [ ] Draw a picture

Name: _______________   Date: _______________

Today is:

| Monday | Tuesday | Wednesday |
| Thursday | Friday | |

Name: ____________________ Date: ____________________

Today is: Monday | Tuesday | Wednesday | Thursday | Friday

Direction: Read the words and make a sentence.

animal den	poule	écuries	dix

ден	кокошка	стаје	десет

____

____

____

____

Name

Draw a Picture

I Can...

☐ use a Capital Letter
The cat is big.

☐ use spaces

☐ sound out words
d-o-g = dog

☐ use a Period .

☐ Draw a picture

Name: _______________________ Date: _______________

Today is:

<table>
<tr><td>Monday</td><td>Tuesday</td><td>Wednesday</td></tr>
<tr><td>Thursday</td><td>Friday</td><td></td></tr>
</table>

Name: _______________________ Date: _______________________

Today is: Monday   Tuesday   Wednesday

Thursday   Friday

Direction: Read the words and make a sentence.

gommeux	maman	somme	tambour
гуми	мама	сума	бубањ

Name

Draw a Picture

I Can...

- [ ] use a Capital Letter
  The cat is big.

- [ ] use spaces

- [ ] sound out words
  d-o-g = dog

- [ ] use a Period .

- [ ] Draw a picture

Name: ___________________   Date: ___________________

Today is: Monday Tuesday Wednesday Thursday Friday

Name: _______________________ Date: _______________

Today is: Monday   Tuesday   Wednesday

Thursday   Friday

Direction: Read the words and make a sentence.

offre	cacher	enfant	couvercle
понуда	сакрити	дете	поклопац

Name

Draw a Picture

I Can...

- [ ] use a Capital Letter
  The cat is big.

- [ ] use spaces

- [ ] sound out words
  d-o-g = dog

- [ ] use a Period .

- [ ] Draw a picture

Name: ___________________ Date: _______________

Today is: Monday Tuesday Wednesday Thursday Friday

Name: _______________________ Date: _______________________

Today is: [Monday] [Tuesday] [Wednesday]
           [Thursday] [Friday]

Direction: Read the words and make a sentence.

gros	creuser	porc	perruque
велика	копати	свиња	перика

____
____

____
____

____
____

____
____

Name

Draw a Picture

I Can...

- [ ] use a Capital Letter
  The cat is big.

- [ ] use spaces

- [ ] sound out words
  d-o-g = dog

- [ ] use a Period .

- [ ] Draw a picture

Name: Date:

Today is: Monday   Tuesday   Wednesday
           Thursday   Friday

Name: ______________________ Date: ______________________

Today is: [Monday] [Tuesday] [Wednesday]
[Thursday] [Friday]

Direction: Read the words and make a sentence.

poubelle	ailette	épingle	gagner
канта	пераја	пин	победити

Name _______________________

Draw a Picture

I Can...

- [ ] use a Capital Letter
  The cat is big.

- [ ] use spaces

- [ ] sound out words
  d-o-g = dog

- [ ] use a Period .

- [ ] Draw a picture

Name: _______________________ Date: _______________

Today is: Monday Tuesday Wednesday Thursday Friday

Name: _______________________ Date: _______________________

Today is:

| Monday | Tuesday | Wednesday |

| Thursday | Friday |

Direction: Read the words and make a sentence.

hanche	lèvres	pincer	boisson
кука	усне	нип	пиће

Name

Draw a Picture

I Can...

☐ use a Capital Letter
<u>T</u>he cat is big.

☐ use spaces

☐ sound out words
d-o-g = dog

☐ use a Period .

☐ Draw a
picture

Name: Date:

Today is: | Monday | Tuesday | Wednesday |
Thursday | Friday |

Name: _______________________ Date: _______________

Today is: Monday Tuesday Wednesday

Thursday Friday

Direction: Read the words and make a sentence.

en forme	frappé	trousse	asseoir
стане	хит	кит	седи

Name ___________________________

Draw a Picture

I Can...

☐ use a Capital Letter
The cat is big.

☐ use spaces

☐ sound out words
d-o-g = dog

☐ use a Period .

☐ Draw a picture

Name: _______________________ Date: _______________

Today is: [Monday] [Tuesday] [Wednesday]
           [Thursday] [Friday]

Name: _________________________ Date: _______________

Today is: | Monday | Tuesday | Wednesday |
| Thursday | Friday |

Direction: Read the words and make a sentence.

blé	emploi	rob	pleurer
кукуруз	посао	опљачкати	плакати

Name

Draw a Picture

I Can...

☐ use a Capital Letter
The cat is big.

☐ use spaces

☐ sound out words
d-o-g = dog

☐ use a Period .

☐ Draw a
picture

Name: Date:

Today is: Monday   Tuesday   Wednesday   Thursday   Friday

Name: _______________________ Date: _______________________

Today is: Monday   Tuesday   Wednesday

Thursday   Friday

Direction: Read the words and make a sentence.

chien	porc	le jogging	bois
пас	свиња	јоггинг	дрво

Name _______________________________

<table>
<tr><td>

Draw a Picture

</td><td>

I Can...

☐ use a Capital Letter
<u>T</u>he cat is big.

☐ use spaces

☐ sound out words
d-o-g = dog

☐ use a Period .

☐ Draw a
picture

</td></tr>
</table>

Name: _______________ Date: _______________

Today is: Monday Tuesday Wednesday
Thursday Friday

Name: _______________   Date: _______________

Today is: [Monday] [Tuesday] [Wednesday]
[Thursday] [Friday]

Direction: Read the words and make a sentence.

punaise	étreinte	cruche	agresser
буг	загрлити	врч	шоља

Name

Draw a Picture

I Can...

- [ ] use a Capital Letter
  The cat is big.

- [ ] use spaces

- [ ] sound out words
  d-o-g = dog

- [ ] use a Period .

- [ ] Draw a picture

Name: ________________ Date: ________________

Today is: Monday   Tuesday   Wednesday
           Thursday   Friday

Name: _______________________ Date: _______________________

Today is: Monday   Tuesday   Wednesday

Thursday   Friday

Direction: Read the words and make a sentence.

lit	point	chaud	pot
кревет	тачка	вруће	лонац

Name

Draw a Picture

I Can...

- [ ] use a Capital Letter
  The cat is big.

- [ ] use spaces

- [ ] sound out words
  d-o-g = dog

- [ ] use a Period .

- [ ] Draw a picture

Name: _____________________ Date: _____________

Today is: Monday Tuesday Wednesday Thursday Friday